# 101 Thematic Poems
# for Emergent Readers

## Lively Rhymes and Easy Activities That Build
## Early Reading Skills and Delight All Learners

SCHOLASTIC
**PROFESSIONAL BOOKS**

New York ★ Toronto ★ London ★ Auckland ★ Sydney ★ Mexico City ★ New Delhi ★ Hong Kong

For my grandsons,
Luc Laplante and Taylor Vida

For one of the finest primary teachers I have known,
my friend and colleague,
Joyce Garneau

And for all of you, my unknown,
colleagues in this great venture...

The poems in the book may be reproduced for classroom use. No other part of this publication may be reproduced in whole or in part or stored in a retrieval system, or transmitted in any form or by any means, electronic, mechanical, photocopying, or otherwise without written permission of the publisher. For information regarding permission, write to Scholastic Inc., 555 Broadway, New York, NY 10012.

Cover design by Jaime Lucero
Interior design by Grafica, Inc.
Illustrations by Amanda Haley

ISBN: 0-590-96733-9
Copyright © 1999 by Mary Sullivan. All rights reserved.
Printed in the U.S.A.

# Table of Contents

Introduction . . . . . . . . . . . . . . . 5
How to Use This Book . . . . . . . . 6
Theme Activities . . . . . . . . . . . 13

## SEASONS AND SPECIAL DAYS

Hello Bus, Yellow Bus . . . . . . . . . 19
Leaves Around the Year . . . . . . 20
Fall Leaves . . . . . . . . . . . . . . 20
Autumn Cheer . . . . . . . . . . . . 21
Winter Cheer . . . . . . . . . . . . . 21
Spring Cheer . . . . . . . . . . . . . 22
Summer Cheer . . . . . . . . . . . . 22
Who Told My Secret? . . . . . . . 23
Rainy Day . . . . . . . . . . . . . . . 24
The Rain Is My Friend . . . . . . . 24
Good Morning, Rainbow . . . . . 25
Spring Fever . . . . . . . . . . . . . . 25
Color Me Cold! . . . . . . . . . . . 26
Building Mr. Snowman . . . . . . . 26
Cloud Parade . . . . . . . . . . . . 27
Wind . . . . . . . . . . . . . . . . . . 27
Birthday Invitation . . . . . . . . . . 28
Halloween Friend . . . . . . . . . . 29
Gift Giving . . . . . . . . . . . . . . . 30
Dear Valentine . . . . . . . . . . . . 31
The 100th Day of School . . . . . 32

## COLOR MY WORLD

Fruits in a Basket . . . . . . . . . . 33
Blue Is . . . . . . . . . . . . . . . . . 34
Green Is . . . . . . . . . . . . . . . . .34
Red Hat . . . . . . . . . . . . . . . . .35
Measles . . . . . . . . . . . . . . . . 35

Yellow Is Warm . . . . . . . . . . . . 36
Purple Shoes . . . . . . . . . . . . . 37
Color Rap . . . . . . . . . . . . . . . 38
Colorful Rainbow . . . . . . . . . . 38
Color My Mood . . . . . . . . . . . 39

## NIFTY NUMBERS

One, Two, Three . . . . . . . . . . . 40
Set It Free . . . . . . . . . . . . . . . 40
What the Little Boy Said . . . . . . 41
Counting by Twos . . . . . . . . . . 42
A Dozen . . . . . . . . . . . . . . . . 42
How Many Legs? . . . . . . . . . . 43
Person Parts . . . . . . . . . . . . . 44
Little Spiders . . . . . . . . . . . . . 44
Giant Dinos . . . . . . . . . . . . . . 45
Mighty Readers . . . . . . . . . . . 45
There Are Two Wheels on a Bike . . 46
One Hundred Days . . . . . . . . . 46
You Can't Count Every Ladybug . 47
Lots and Lots of People . . . . . . 47

## LOOK AT ME NOW!

When I Was a Baby . . . . . . . . . 48
Growing . . . . . . . . . . . . . . . . 49
Look What I Drew! . . . . . . . . . . 49
Haircut . . . . . . . . . . . . . . . . . 50
One or Two . . . . . . . . . . . . . . 50
Pocket Treasure . . . . . . . . . . . 51
To Be Six . . . . . . . . . . . . . . . . 52
Smiles Go 'Round . . . . . . . . . . 52
The Race . . . . . . . . . . . . . . . . 53
Eyes to See . . . . . . . . . . . . . . 53

*continued on next page*

Finger Wise . . . . . . . . . . . . . . . 54
The Nose Knows . . . . . . . . . . . . 54
I Spy (A Rose) . . . . . . . . . . . . 55
Sounds All Around . . . . . . . . . . 55

## PEOPLE, PLACES, TRUCKS, AND TRIKES

Home Sweet Home . . . . . . . . . . 56
A Trip to the Zoo . . . . . . . . . . 57
I'd Like to Have a Treehouse . . . 58
Paul and Pete and Patty, Too . . 59
Sandbox . . . . . . . . . . . . . . . . 59
At the Pool . . . . . . . . . . . . . . . 60
Bikes and Trikes . . . . . . . . . . . 60
Did You See the Jet Plane? . . . . 61
So Big, So Small . . . . . . . . . . . 61
Wheels on a Train . . . . . . . . . . 61

## FAVORITE FOODS

Breakfast on the Farm . . . . . . . . 62
At the Grocery Store . . . . . . . . 62
A Trip to the Fruit Stand . . . . . . 63
Fruit Riddle . . . . . . . . . . . . . . . 63
Silly Sandwich . . . . . . . . . . . . 64
I Really Love My Veggies . . . . . . 64
What the Popcorn Said . . . . . . 65
Pizza Time . . . . . . . . . . . . . . . 65
At the Ice-Cream Shop . . . . . . 66
Ice-Cream Dream . . . . . . . . . . 66
Let Me Dream of Peanut Butter . . 67

## ANIMALS, ANIMALS

Do You Have a Pet? . . . . . . . . 68

My Cousin Has White Mice . . . . . 69
Bear-ly Awake . . . . . . . . . . . . 69
Summer Bunny, Winter Bunny . . . 70
Dog, Bird, Turtle, Bat . . . . . . . . 70
Farm Families . . . . . . . . . . . . . 71
Farm Riddles . . . . . . . . . . . . . 72
More Farm Riddles . . . . . . . . . . 73
Five Little Ducklings . . . . . . . . . 74
Green, Green Frog . . . . . . . . . . 74
I Spy (A Mouse) . . . . . . . . . . . 75
Little Mouse, Little Mouse . . . . . . 75
The Robin's Secret . . . . . . . . . . 76
Pelican Pouch . . . . . . . . . . . . 76
The Peacock's Tail . . . . . . . . . . 77
Tadpoles . . . . . . . . . . . . . . . . 77
Mom's Allergic . . . . . . . . . . . . 78
Animal Homes . . . . . . . . . . . . 79
A Dinosaur Was at My Door . . . . 80

## CREEPY CRAWLIES

Beetle Has His Beetle Ways . . . . . 81
Butterfly, Flutter By . . . . . . . . . . 82
Caterpillar Small . . . . . . . . . . . 82
Summer Surprise . . . . . . . . . . . 83
Mr. Bumblebee . . . . . . . . . . . . 83
I Spy (A Grasshopper) . . . . . . . . 84
I Spy (A Bee) . . . . . . . . . . . . . 84
The Tiny World . . . . . . . . . . . . 85
The Ladybug's Coat . . . . . . . . . 85
Mosquito . . . . . . . . . . . . . . . . 86
Spider Friends . . . . . . . . . . . . 86
Webs in the Grass . . . . . . . . . . 87
Wiggly Worm . . . . . . . . . . . . . 87

# Introduction

## Dear Teachers,

Children, like many adults, are fascinated by language. They delight in humorous, interesting, and delicious words just for the fun of hearing and saying them. The joy and excitement you have for language will affect the literature you share with your students. Listening to stories and poems read aloud provides children preparation and motivation for reading by introducing them to the functions and forms of print, building their oral vocabularies, and sparking their imaginations.

For over 30 years, I have used poems as a key part of my literacy curriculum. Poems offer great opportunities for the direct teaching of emergent reading skills. The lyrical quality, playful language, and frequent repetition in poetry draw my students into a world of sounds, words, and ideas and enable me to focus on the connection between spoken and written language.

I wrote the poems in this book for use with popular primary-grade themes such as colors, numbers, seasons, animals, holidays, and friends. The patterned, repetitive nature of the poems is a great aid to emergent readers because it allows them to feel successful and develop early reading fluency.

I have included poems like "Webs in the Grass" and "The Peacock's Tail" to provide an opportunity for sharing figurative language with children. The poems "Dear Valentine" and "Color My Mood" create occasions to talk about feelings and emotions. Some of the poems feature onomatopoetic words and strong sound patterns such as "Sounds All Around" and "Hello Bus, Yellow Bus." Other are pure fun such as "Dinosaur at My Door" and "Mom's Alllergic." But all of the poetry allows children to experience the beauty, power, and fun of language. I share these poems with you so that you can achieve the same.

A child's literacy development is supported by a literature-rich environment. Children come to school with some capacity for spoken language. We want to show them that print represents the spoken words they already know. We also want to have them look at print carefully, critically, and often; help them notice differences between letters and words; and support them in noticing that certain sounds are represented by specific letters and letter combinations. The poems and activities that follow will allow you to accomplish these and other early literacy goals.

The challenge of nurturing children's literacy growth is a daunting one given the demands on educators and the lack of readiness for reading among many children. Nevertheless, learning to read remains the most important factor in the fulfillment of individual potential in our society. To have even the smallest part in such a grand accomplishment is our greatest reward in this work we call teaching. I hope that *101 Thematic Poems for Emergent Readers* provides some assistance by enhancing your literature collection as you embark on the important task of teaching your students to read. I wish you much success.

Enjoy!

Mary Sullivan

# How to Use This Book

## Introducing the Poems

You can bring each poem to life by sharing your enthusiasm about the poem's language and content. In addition, when introducing each poem I suggest the following routine.

1 Write the poem on chart paper. Poems should be written in large print for easy viewing by students. You may wish to laminate the charts so you can write on and reuse them. As an alternative, make a transparency of the poem and show it on an overhead projector. You might also distribute individual photocopies of the poem to children.

2 Read aloud the poem for children to enjoy. Add movements and vary the tone or pace of your reading when appropriate.

3 Then, reread the poem aloud as you track the print. Always read aloud the poem one or more times before inviting students to join in on the reading.

4 On a final reading, do one or all of the following:

• Have children join in on the repetitive parts of the poem.

• Have children point out rhyming words, or words that begin with a target sound, such as /s/. Then, frame the words as you reread. Have children clap every time you read one of the framed words. Or, pause before the words and let children provide them.

• Have children clap the rhythm of the poem as you read it aloud.

• Have children highlight interesting words they hear or see in the poem. Add these words to a word wall for children to use when reading and writing.

5 Introduce the accompanying activities.

## General Tips and Activities

To get the most instructional benefits from the poems, I suggest the following activities that focus on emergent reading skills.

✮ **Innovate on the text.** Substitute poem words. For example, using a self-sticking note, substitute the first word in a rhyming pair. Children then suggest a rhyming word to replace the second word in the pair. Write the word on a self-sticking note and place it in the appropriate place in the poem. Help children read the "new" poem.

✮ **Add hand motions or movements.** These movements can liven up rereadings. For example, have children perform the actions mentioned in each line

of "At the Pool," point to the appropriate spot when reading "Person Parts," or change their facial expressions when reading "Color My Mood."

✯ **Use the poems as springboards for writing.** Create charts of theme-related poem words or poem words containing a specific letter or phonogram. Use these charts for shared or interactive writing assignments. During interactive writing, "share the pen" with students by asking them to write specific words or word parts in the story you create as a class.

✯ **Photocopy and reuse the poems.** The poems can be sent home for a shared reading experience with family members, or used in the classroom for paired or choral reading. You may also use the poems for search activities. During search activities, have students circle all the words with a specific sound-spelling, or words that rhyme.

✯ **Make sentence strips for each poem.** Place the sentence strips in a large pocket chart in random order. As you read aloud the poem, have students find the corresponding sentence strip and place it in the correct order in the pocket chart. Use the sentence strips for one-to-one matching and for discussing concepts of print such as directionality, left-to-right progression, return sweeps, capitalization, and punctuation.

✯ **Record the poems.** Place the audio-cassette recordings in a listening center. Invite students to listen to the poems during independent or center time. Students may wish to draw a picture illustrating a poem or write a sentence telling about it. Students may also wish to make their own recordings of the poems. Encourage them to use instruments to accompany their recordings.

✯ **Use the poems for reader's theater.** Assign poems to pairs or small groups of students. Provide time for students to practice and present their readings. Help students with proper phrasing, tone, pacing, and volume while preparing for their presentations.

✯ **Use the poems for cloze activities.** During cloze activities, cover specific poem words for students to provide during the reading. If students provide related words, analyze the words in terms of meaning and form. For example, ask students what letters the two words begin with or how the words are the same.

✯ **Use the poems to develop and expand vocabulary.** Children are exposed to words like "fawn" and "kale." They encounter the names of animals, insects, and even vegetables that are new to them.

✯ **Use the poems to create links to other literature.** The poems can provide clues to the interests of your students. If students respond favorably to the content of a particular poem, present them with related literature that will hook them as readers. For example, after reading a poem about bugs, one student may move on to a nonfiction book, while another to a collection of nonsense verse. Such links will support young readers as they become empowered by the skills they gain, are given opportunities to use their literacy skills, as well as when they read for specific purposes, experience literature and functional print firsthand, and have their reading successes celebrated.

✯ **Use prompts and questions while students read to help them focus on and apply their knowledge of phonics skills.**

- Find all of the words that begin with the letter ____. (*end with the letter*)
- Pick a word and tell me what sound you hear at the beginning. (*at the end*)
- Find a word that begins with the sound you hear at the beginning of _____. (*ends with*)
- Find a word that rhymes with _____.
- How many words begin with the _____ sound? What are they? (*end with*)
- Find all of the words that contain

the _____ sound *[say a long or short vowel sound]*. This is the sound you hear in the word _____.

✯ **Use the poems to introduce key phonics skills.** Browse the book. Select a poem that fits your instructional needs. Note the theme and phonics skill associated with each poem. Then, use the poem to introduce or review skills. For example, for phonemic awareness practice have children listen for words with a target sound as you read the poem aloud. Then, have them generate other words with that sound. On the following pages you will find a skills matrix which details the phonics and phonemic awareness skills highlighted in each poem.

# Skills Matrix

| POEM TITLE | short vowel | long vowel | variant vowel | consonant | consonant digraph | consonant cluster |
|---|---|---|---|---|---|---|
| Hello Bus, Yellow Bus, p. 19 | u | a, o | | y | | |
| Leaves Around the Year, p. 20 | | e | | | | r-blend |
| Fall Leaves, p. 20 | | i | | | | s-blend |
| Autumn Cheer, p. 21 | | | | | ch | |
| Winter Cheer, p. 21 | | | | | | r-blend |
| Spring Cheer, p. 22 | | a | | p | | |
| Summer Cheer, p. 22 | | | | | | s-blend |
| Who Told My Secret?, p. 23 | | e | | | | l-blend |
| Rainy Day, p. 24 | i, o | a | | | | l-blend |
| The Rain Is My Friend, p. 24 | | | | c | | |
| Good Morning, Rainbow, p. 25 | | silent e | | | | |
| Spring Fever, p. 25 | | e | | f | | |
| Color Me Cold!, p. 26 | | o | | | | |
| Building Mr. Snowman, p. 26 | | | /ô/ | b | | |
| Cloud Parade, p. 27 | | | | | | l-blend |
| Wind, p. 27 | | | | | | r-blend |
| Birthday Invitation, p. 28 | u | | | | | |
| Halloween Friend, p. 29 | | i | | | | |
| Gift Giving, p. 30 | i | | | g,/s/,c | | |
| Dear Valentine, p. 31 | | | | v | th | |
| The 100th Day of School, p. 32 | u | e | | | | |
| Fruits in a Basket, p. 33 | | e | /ou/ | l | | |
| Blue Is, p. 34 | | a | | | | l-blend |
| Green Is, p. 34 | | e | | | | |
| Red Hat, p. 35 | a, e | | | | | |
| Measles, p. 35 | e | | | | | |
| Yellow Is Warm, p. 36 | i | i, o | | y | | |
| Purple Shoes, p. 37 | | o | r-controlled | b, r | | |

# Skills Matrix

| POEM TITLE | short vowel | long vowel | variant vowel | con-sonant | consonant digraph | consonant cluster |
|---|---|---|---|---|---|---|
| Color Rap, p. 38 | a | i, o | | | | |
| Colorful Rainbow, p. 38 | e | | | | | |
| Color My Mood, p. 39 | e | | | | wh | |
| One, Two, Three, p. 40 | | e, silent e | | | | |
| Set It Free, p. 40 | | silent e | | | | |
| What the Little Boy Said, p. 41 | e | | | x | | |
| Counting by Twos, p. 42 | i | | r-con-trolled | | | |
| A Dozen, p. 42 | | | | z | th | |
| How Many Legs?, p. 43 | a, e | | | | | s-blend |
| Person Parts, p. 44 | | o | | t | | |
| Little Spiders, p. 44 | i | | | l | | s-blend |
| Giant Dinos, p. 45 | | | | d, g | | |
| Mighty Readers, p. 45 | | i | | r | | |
| There Are Two Wheels on a Bike, p. 46 | | | | | th | |
| One Hundred Days, p. 46 | | | | h | | |
| You Can't Count Every Ladybug, p. 47 | | | /ou/ | c | | r-blend |
| Lots and Lots of People, p. 47 | | | /ou/ | t | | |
| When I Was a Baby, p. 48 | | | r-con-trolled | | | |
| Growing, p. 49 | | o | | | | |
| Look What I Drew!, p. 49 | | | | | | r-blend |
| Haircut, p. 50 | | | r-con-trolled | | | |
| One or Two, p. 50 | | i, silent e | | | | |
| Pocket Treasure, p. 51 | i | | | ck | | |
| To Be Six, p. 52 | | i | | n | | |
| Smiles Go 'Round, p. 52 | | i | | h | | |
| The Race, p. 53 | u | | | | | |
| Eyes to See, p. 53 | u | e | | s | | |
| Finger Wise, p. 54 | u | | | | | |

# Skills Matrix

| POEM TITLE | short vowel | long vowel | variant vowel | con-sonant | consonant digraph | consonant cluster |
|---|---|---|---|---|---|---|
| The Nose Knows, p. 54 | | o | | v | | l-blend |
| I Spy (A Rose), p. 55 | | | | s | th | s-blend |
| Sounds All Around, p. 55 | i | e | | | ch | s-blend |
| Home Sweet Home, p. 56 | | a, o | /ou/ | | | |
| A Trip to the Zoo, p. 57 | | a | | | wh | |
| I'd Like to Have a Treehouse, p. 58 | | i | | h | | |
| Paul and Pete and Patty, Too, p. 59 | | | /ʃ/ | p | | |
| Sandbox, p. 59 | | | r-con-trolled | s | | |
| At the Pool, p. 60 | | | /ʃ/ | | th | s-blend |
| Bikes and Trikes, p. 60 | | silent e | | | | |
| Did You See the Jet Plane?, p. 61 | | i | | j | | |
| So Big, So Small, p. 61 | | i | | j | | |
| Wheels on a Train, p. 61 | | e | | v | | |
| Breakfast on the Farm, p. 62 | | e | r-con-trolled | | ch | |
| At the Grocery Store, p. 62 | | e | | p | | |
| A Trip to the Fruit Stand, p. 63 | | | /ʃ/ | | | |
| Fruit Riddle, p. 63 | | e | r-con-trolled | | | |
| Silly Sandwich, p. 64 | | | | l | | |
| I Really Love My Veggies, p. 64 | u | | | | | |
| What the Popcorn Said, p. 65 | o | | /ou/ | | | |
| Pizza Time, p. 65 | | i | | s | | |
| At the Ice-Cream Shop, p. 66 | | | | | ch | |
| Ice-Cream Dream, p. 66 | | e | | | | |
| Let Me Dream of Peanut Butter, p. 67 | u | | | b | | |
| Do You Have a Pet?, p. 68 | e, u | | r-con-trolled | d | | |
| My Cousin Has White Mice, p. 69 | i | | | | | |
| Bear-ly Awake, p. 69 | | | /ʃ/ | | | |
| Summer Bunny, Winter Bunny, p. 70 | u | o | | b | | |

# Skills Matrix

| POEM TITLE | short vowel | long vowel | variant vowel | con- sonant | consonant digraph | consonant cluster |
|---|---|---|---|---|---|---|
| Dog, Bird, Turtle, Bat, p. 70 | | | /ô/ | l, p | | |
| Farm Families, p. 71 | | | | f | th | |
| Farm Riddles, p. 72 | | | r-con- trolled | b, p | | |
| More Farm Riddles, p. 73 | | | /ʃ/ | | | |
| Five Little Ducklings, p. 74 | | o | | f | | l-blend |
| Green, Green Frog, p. 74 | | | | z | | r-blend l-blend |
| I Spy (A Mouse), p. 75 | | e | | s | | |
| Little Mouse, Little Mouse, p. 75 | | | /ou/ | l, m | | |
| The Robin's Secret, p. 76 | | e | | | | |
| Pelican Pouch, p. 76 | i | | | p | | |
| The Peacock's Tail, p. 77 | | | | p | | |
| Tadpoles, p. 77 | e | o | | | | r-blend |
| Mom's Allergic, p. 78 | i | /yʃ/ | | | | s-blend |
| Animal Homes, p. 79 | | | | b | | |
| A Dinosaur Was at My Door, p. 80 | | | | c | | |
| Beetle Has His Beetle Ways, p. 81 | | e | r-con- trolled | b | | |
| Butterfly, Flutter By, p. 82 | a | | | f | | |
| Caterpillar Small, p. 82 | | | /ô/ | | | |
| Summer Surprise, p. 83 | | i | | t | | |
| Mr. Bumblebee, p. 83 | | o | | b | | |
| I Spy (A Grasshopper), p. 84 | i | i | | | | r-blend |
| I Spy (A Bee), p. 84 | | | | f, y | | |
| The Tiny World, p. 85 | a, e | e | /ô/ | | | r-blend |
| The Ladybug's Coat, p. 85 | a | | | | | |
| Mosquito, p. 86 | | | | /s/, c | | s-blend r-blend |
| Spider Friends, p. 86 | | | | | | |
| Webs in the Grass, p. 87 | | i | r-con- trolled | l | | |
| Wiggly Worm, p. 87 | | | r-con- trolled | w | | |

# Theme Activities

## Seasons and Special Days

✯ As each holiday approaches, read the corresponding poem and use it as a springboard for holiday-related art and writing projects. For example, "Halloween Friend" can be an introduction to writing scary stories, making orange and black paper jack-o-lanterns, designing costumes, and other spooky or fun holiday activities.

✯ Start a seasons booklet at the beginning of the school year. During each season, photocopy the appropriate poem and have students paste it into their own seasons booklets. As the season progresses, periodically ask students to add season-related poems, stories, and art projects. In addition, students may wish to add realia (objects, articles, etc.) associated with each season, such as pressed leaves and football banners during autumn, or flowers and rainy-day weather reports during spring.

✯ Use the season poems as homework reading during a science unit on the seasons, weather, or earth's rotation. Ask students to connect science concepts to the content of each related poem.

✯ After reading the poems "Rainy Day," "The Rain Is My Friend," or "Color Me Cold!," have students collect data and present daily weather reports. You might assign one or more students each day of the month. The students can watch the local news reports or clip the weather forecast from a newspaper. Have students record their data on a weather-reporting form and gather the pages for a yearly weather book. Suggest that students read a weather-related poem such as one from this book to begin or end their oral weather reports.

✯ The poem "the 100th Day of School" celebrates the 100th day of school. To prepare for this day, keep a running tally of each day of school across the top of your chalkboard. You may wish to write the tens in one color and the ones in another color to highlight them. Plan a 100th-day celebration using the poem and other related books such as *Exploring the Numbers 1 to 100* (Scholastic), *The Celebrate 100 Kit* (Scholastic), and *The 100th Day of School* (by Angela Shelf Medearis).

## Color My World

✯ Use the color poems as a springboard to studying the colors of the rainbow. Children can create a rainbow booklet, copying a poem from this book about a color of the rainbow, or creating a poem for each color. Introduce children to the acronym ROY G. BIV to help them remember the colors of the rainbow and explore the scientific reasons rainbows occur.

✯ Have children select a favorite color and write a color poem beginning with the words "(*Name of color*) is . . ." See below for a sample. Encourage children to choose interesting or unusual color names such as forest green, aqua, or burnt orange.

> Red is . . .
> Red is like a ruby shining brightly.
> Red is the color of apples falling from a tree.
> Red is mama's lipstick when she first puts it on.

✯ For each poem, have students find and record related color words. For example, for the color "blue" students might record teal, aquamarine, and navy. Create color-word webs and display them in a writing center for students to use when writing.

✯ Have students write their own color raps using "Color Rap" as a model. Suggest that they record their raps using any instruments they wish to accompany the songs. Have students perform their raps for the class.

✯ Poll students about their favorite colors and work as a class to create a favorite-colors graph. Use the graph to teach children how to get information from graphic aids. Then, copy or produce other graphs (bar graphs, pie graphs, etc.) and place them in a math center. Write questions about each graph on large index cards and attach to the appropriate graph. Write the answers on the back of each card so students can self-check their work.

## Nifty Numbers

✯ Select and photocopy one of the number poems, such as "Counting by Twos" or "How Many Legs?" On the back of the poem, have students create word problems for classmates to solve. For example, "2 + 2 + 2 = ___" or "How many total legs do three children have?" You may wish to have students write a few sentences telling the methods they used to solve the problems.

✯ Use the poems as springboards for math activities. For example, after reading "Counting by Twos" have the students count by twos as they walk in line to lunch or recess. On what number do they arrive at their destination? Or, after reading "Giant Dinos" have students practice counting using hopscotch boards. Write the appropriate number on each square of the hopscotch board. Then, call out a number problem such as "2 dinos plus 1 dino" or "11 minus 7" and have students hop to the correct number on the board.

✯ To practice counting to or by a dozen after reading the poem "A Dozen," use empty egg cartons. For example, for counting to a dozen, cut several cartons into small sections, each containing a different number of egg holders. Mix the

14

cartons and have students find two or more that add up to a dozen.

✶ After reading "Mighty Readers," count and graph the number of objects in your classroom. To begin, select four or five objects such as desks, chairs, televisions, chalkboards, and computers. Have students create a graph showing the number of each object. Then, create or have students create questions to ask about the graph.

✶ Create a math "problem of the day." Place the problem in a pocket chart. Have students try to solve the problem throughout the day. Students can place their answers on slips of paper (along with their names) in a can next to the pocket chart. At the end of the day, reveal the answer. You may select a slip of paper and have that student explain how he or she solved the problem. Periodically, replace the problem of the day with a math poem for students to enjoy and practice reading.

## Look at Me Now!

✶ Have students create an autobiographical booklet. On each page, ask them to write an age from one to their current age. Under each number, have them draw pictures showing key events that happened during that year of their life. They might also want to add mementos such as copies of photographs or stories they have written.

Have them add their favorite poem from this book to their booklet.

✶ After reading "Look What I Drew!," provide students with large sheets of mural paper. Have each student lie down on the paper while a partner traces his or her body outline. Then, have students draw pictures inside the outline that tell about themselves. For example, a student might draw a baseball bat because he likes playing baseball, a picture of his family, and pictures of his favorite foods.

✶ Connect the poems "Look What I Drew!" and "Smiles Go 'Round" to a unit on emotions. Generate a list of emotion words such as happy, sad, giggly, angry, and shy. Write the emotion words on index cards. Have students draw pictures on other index cards illustrating each emotion, one picture per card. Use the cards to play a game of Concentration.

✶ Connect the poems "When I Was a Baby," "Eyes to See," and "The Nose Knows" to science units on how the body works. Use the poems as introductions to the unit, or assign them for home reading.

## People, Places, Trucks, and Trikes

✶ Take a walk with students around your neighborhood. Have them take

photographs or sketch pictures of the things they see. When you return to the classroom, distribute large sheets of mural paper. Have students draw neighborhood scenes on the paper. As an alternative, have students draw scenes of places you've visited on field trips, such as the zoo or aquarium. Display the murals in the school hallway. Attach copies of related poems, such as "A Trip to the Zoo" or "Home Sweet Home" for passersby to enjoy.

✯ Have students draw or make a diorama of special places they would like to create for themselves or their friends. Have students write a poem about their dioramas using "I'd Like to Have a Treehouse" as a model. Provide time for students to share their poems and dioramas.

✯ After reading the poems in this section, locate and display photographs of interesting places around the world. Introduce students to descriptive words about these places. Write the words on chart paper. Place the pictures and chart paper in a writing center. Have students write about *their* favorite places.

✯ Connect poems such as "Did You See the Jet Plane?" to a transportation unit. Have students draw pictures of the many forms of transportation mentioned in the poem. Suggest that they add other forms of transportation they have seen or read about. Then, create a bulletin-board dis-

play using the pictures and related poems. To create the display, have students categorize the types of transportation—land, water, air—and find the most appropriate poems for each.

## Favorite Foods

✯ Poll students about their favorite foods. Then, work together to create a pie graph using the data. To extend the activity, have students interview friends and family members about their favorite foods and create a pie or bar graph illustrating the information collected.

✯ After reading "Silly Sandwich," have students collect favorite recipes. Ask them to write the recipes on large index cards or colored construction paper. Suggest that they add a picture or photo of the completed dish. Gather the recipes to create a class book.

✯ Connect the poems "Fruit Riddle" and "I Really Love My Veggies" to class cooking experiences. Share the poems while students enjoy the results of their cooking.

✯ Have students create a menu for a nutritious meal. Introduce students to the basic food groups and display the food group distribution chart for student reference. Have students share their menus and ask classmates to evaluate their nutritional value.

✯ Turn a corner of your classroom into

a restaurant. Stock the corner with student-created menus, plastic food, play money, sample bills, and tables with tablecloths and other items. Have students take the role of waiter/waitress or patron. Use this as an opportunity to reinforce reading and math skills. Place food-related poems and books in the restaurant for patrons to read while waiting for their food to be served.

## Animals, Animals

✯ Have students collect pictures of animals that interest them. Use the poems to spark ideas. You may wish to generate a list of animals on the chalkboard, or display animal books for students to find animal names. Then, help students write mini reports about animals of their choice. You might also wish to have students create animal-fact cards, much like baseball cards. On one side of an index card, have students write three facts about their chosen animals. On the other side, have them draw or cut out a picture of the animals.

✯ After reading "Do You Have a Pet?" have students describe a special pet they have or would like to have. You may wish to have students write a poem about the pet using "Do You Have a Pet?" as a model.

✯ After reading several animal poems, have students create imaginary animals. For example, one might combine an ele-

phant and a giraffe to create an elephaffe. Have them illustrate their new animals and write poems about them using "Green, Green Frog" as a model.

✯ After reading a poem such as "The Peacock's Tail," have students select an animal and write a porquoi tale about it. For example, they might write about why peacocks have colorful feathers, why turtles have shells, how zebras got their stripes, or how leopards got their spots. To help students, gather and read a few porquoi tales, such as those by Rudyard Kipling, to stimulate ideas.

✯ Display pictures of animals. Have students categorize the animal pictures in any way they choose. They might categorize them by number of legs, type of skin (fur, feathers, scales), or size.

✯ After reading a poem such as "Farm Families," show a video about the animals mentioned. Have students compare the information in the poem to that in the video. What new information did they acquire? What can they learn about animals from other sources such as: zoo visits, encyclopedias, and interviewing veterinarians?

✯ Connect the reading of poems such as "Tadpoles," "Animal Homes," or "Farm Families" to a study of animal life cycles, animal homes, or animal communities. Have students copy the poems

onto larger sheets of colored construction paper and illustrate them with pictures or diagrams showing the information learned.

✦ Have students collect data about animals in their environment. Ask students to select three animals to observe throughout the week. Suggest that they create a mini field guide to record their data, including drawings of the animals in their habitats. Remind students that many animals live in unusual places, such as birds living in nests in the nooks of skyscrapers. Encourage students to locate and observe these and other animals.

## Creepy Crawlies

✦ Make an ant farm for your class to observe. Ant farms can be purchased at many toy or specialty stores. Before beginning the ant farm, read aloud the poem "The Tiny World" and other literature about ants and other insects. Focus on the ways in which insects work together to create their communities. Connect this system to the ways in which people work together in their communities.

✦ After reading any of the poems in this section, read aloud other insect-related books to expand students' knowledge base and vocabulary. Ask students to select an insect of interest and create a large papier-mâché rendering of it. Hang the insects from the ceiling for a

"buggy" classroom environment.

✦ After reading "Butterfly, Flutter By" and "Caterpillar Small," study the life cycle of the butterfly. Introduce words such as caterpillar, cocoon, chrysalis, and pupa. Have students create a poster showing the life cycle. Students may also wish to study and create life-cycle posters for other animals.

✦ Connect the reading of poems such as "Mr. Bumblebee," "Webs in the Grass," or "I Spy" to the study of the roles of insects in the animal world. The roles might include the importance of bees in pollination or how some insects eat other insects that threaten crops. Help students collect information about the importance of these animals in the life cycles of plants.

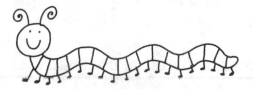

## Hello Bus, Yellow Bus

Hello bus, yellow bus,
Wait, wait, wait!

Hello bus, yellow bus,
I'm late, late, late!

Hello bus, yellow bus,
One minute more!

Hello bus, yellow bus,
Open up your door!

Hello bus, yellow bus,
Now, I'm on my way!

Hello bus, good-fellow bus
You really saved the day!

## Leaves Around the Year

In spring the leaves
Are clean and bright.

They green and grow
In summer's light.

In fall they turn
To red and gold.

Then curl up brown
In winter's cold.

## Fall Leaves

I like the leaves in fall,
I like their colors bright.
Gold and orange, yellow, red—
What a splendid sight!

I like the leaves in fall,
The way they crunch beneath my feet,
Then whisper 'round the driveway
And scatter down the street.

## Autumn Cheer

I love all the seasons,
But autumn is the best!
Let's put on our sweaters,
Now we are all dressed.
In the leaves, we love to play
And this is what we hear:
Crunch, crunch, crunch, crunch!
That's this season's cheer!

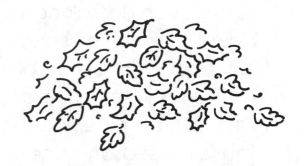

## Winter Cheer

I love all the seasons,
But winter is the best!
Let's put on our mittens,
Now we are all dressed.
In the snow, we love to play
And this is what we hear:
Brrr, brrr, brrr, brrr!
That's this season's cheer!

## Spring Cheer

I love all the seasons,
But springtime is the best!
Let's put on our raincoats,
Now we are all dressed.
In the rain, we love to play
And this is what we hear:
Pitter, patter, pitter, patter!
That's this season's cheer!

## Summer Cheer

I love all the seasons,
But summer is the best!
Let's put on our swimsuits,
Now we are all dressed.
In the pool, we love to play
And this is what we hear:
Splish, splash, splish splash!
That's this season's cheer!

# Who Told My Secret?

I told my secret to a sparrow in a tree.
The sparrow told a blossom.
The blossom told a bee.

The bee told a flower
In the soft summer grass.
The flower told a gentle breeze
Just happening to pass.

The breeze told a gray cloud
That was floating in the air.
Then, down came the rain
And spread it everywhere!

## Rainy Day

Plip! Plop!
Raindrop.
I'll stay inside today.

Plip! Plop!
Raindrop.
I'll call a friend to play.

Plip! Plop!
Raindrop.
I know my friend will say:

"Plip! Plop!
Raindrop.
We'll have fun today!"

## The Rain Is My Friend

The rain is my friend
'Cause when it comes
Ditches fill and water runs!

Out I go
In boots and coat
To sail my little plastic boat.

In puddles deep, I slosh all day
And with my friend,
I play and play!

## Good Morning, Rainbow

Good morning, rainbow,
You make the rain worthwhile!

Good morning, rainbow,
You're an upside down smile!

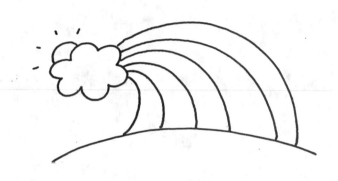

## Spring Fever

I'm feeling oh-so silly,
I'm really in a muddle.
Can it be spring fever
That
    puts
       my
          feet
            in
              every
                puddle?

## Color Me Cold!

Red cheeks,
White toes,
Blue fingers—
Red nose!

## Building Mr. Snowman

Head ball,
Belly ball,
Bottom ball—
Done!

Building Mr. Snowman
Is always lots of fun!

## Cloud Parade

When I lie on my back
And watch the sky
A cloud parade
Goes drifting by:

Lions and tigers
And elephants too—
A dinosaur's playing
A puffy kazoo.

There are dogs and fish
And castles that fade
In my silent, floating
Cloud parade.

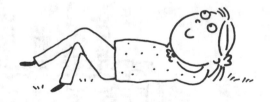

## Wind

I'd love to be a summer wind—
A soft warm breeze,
Bending the heads of buttercups
And whispering to the leaves.

# Birthday Invitation

Please come to my birthday,
We're going to have such fun!
I'll feed you cake and ice cream
And a hot dog on a bun!

Please come to my birthday,
We're going to have such fun!
Of all the friends invited,
You're such a special one!

## Halloween Friend

Orange Mr. Pumpkinhead,
The window frames your grin.
Long after I have gone to bed,
Your candle burns within.

I worked so hard to carve your mouth,
Those circles for your eyes.
And now you light this special night—
A Halloween surprise!

# Gift Giving

It's nice, when gifts are given,
If something is for me.

But an even better gift
Is the one for YOU from me.

I saved up lots of money,
I wrapped it by myself.

I hope that you will like it
And place it on a shelf.

It's fun to have a secret,
A fancy wrapped surprise.

I know that you're excited,
I see it in your eyes!

## Dear Valentine

I have for you a valentine
That's special as can be.
It's so unique a valentine
It could only be from me.

It's better than chocolates,
Or flowers, or a rhyme.
It's made from something precious
That you've had for quite some time.

This valentine says plainly
I LOVE YOU.
This valentine says thank you
for the ways you love me too.

My valentine's an open heart
That's trimmed around with lace.
My valentine's a heart that's filled
With my smiling face!

# The 100th Day of School

Celebrate 100 days—
It has been quite a year!
We've learned so much and had such fun,
Let's give ourselves a cheer!

It's great to see what each friend brings
To show one hundred things:
One hundred pennies, buttons, seeds,
One hundred colored beads.

One hundred days of counting
And of reading story books,
One hundred days of songs and rhymes,
Of jackets hung on hooks.

Celebrate 100 days—
It has been quite a year!
We've learned so much and had such fun,
Let's give ourselves a cheer!

# Fruits in a Basket

Yellow
Little lemon,
Sour as can be!

Green
Little apple,
Picked from the tree!

Purple
Little plum,
You're juicy and round!

Blue
Little berries,
Grown on the ground!

Red
Little cherries,
Sweet, very sweet!

Orange
Little peach,
So good to eat!

## Blue Is

Blue is the color of the morning sky.
Blue are the berries in a blueberry pie.

Blue is the color of a summer lake.
Blue is the icing on my birthday cake.

Blue is the color of the wings of a jay.
Blue am I when I can't go out to play!

## Green Is

Green is a frog
A lime, and a tree.

Green is a jelly bean
And Japanese tea.

Green is a hillside,
A pickle, and the sea.

I'd say green is lovely
If you ask me!

## Red Hat

Red hat, red hair,
Red mat, red chair.

Red bug, red spot,
Red rug, red dots.

Red face, red feather,
Red lace, red leather.

Red nose, red mitt,
Red rose, let's quit!

## Measles

Red nose,
Red eyes,
Red spots—
SURPRISE!

## Yellow Is Warm

Yellow is warm,
Yellow is light,
Yellow is the color of buttercups bright.

Yellow is a lemon
And a daisy dot,
Yellow is the sun when the day is super hot.

Yellow is warm,
Yellow is bright,
Five fluffy chicks—oh, what a sight!

# Purple Shoes

Gary has a green hat,
Green so fine.
Gary has a green hat
Just like mine.

Bonnie has a blue sweater,
Blue so fine.
Bonnie has a blue sweater,
Just like mine.

Robert has a red coat,
Red so fine.
Robert has a red coat,
Just like mine.

Yolanda has a yellow shirt,
Yellow so fine.
Yolanda has a yellow shirt,
Just like mine.

Brian has some brown pants,
Brown so fine.
Brian has some brown pants,
Just like mine.

I have some purple shoes,
Purple so fine.
And no one has shoes,
Quite like mine!

## Color Rap

Yellow, yellow,
Lemon Jell-o.

Red, red,
Poppy head.

Black, black,
Beetle back.

White, white,
Stars at night.

Green, green,
Jelly bean.

Blue, blue,
Missing you!

## Colorful Rainbow

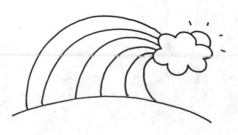

Yellow, red, green, purple, blue—
All the colors bend.
Some say that a pot of gold
Is at the very end!

## Color My Mood

Colors name the way we feel,
When we're angry or we're sad:

I'm blue when I'm lonely,
I'm red when I'm mad.

I'm green when I'm jealous,
I'm pink when I'm glad.

I'm orange when I'm good,
I'm purple when I'm bad.

And I made up a new name
For when I'm feeling mellow.

I'm think I'm gonna call it:
Lemon Jell-o yellow!

## One, Two, Three

One, two, three,
Ice cream just for me!

Four, five, six,
I'll take a couple licks!

Seven, eight, nine,
It really tastes divine!

Ten, ten, ten,
Time to count again!

## Set It Free

One, two, three, four, five,
Catch a fly alive!
Six, seven, eight, nine, ten,
Set it free again!

One, two, three, four, five,
Catch a frog alive!
Six, seven, eight, nine, ten,
Set it free again!

One, two, three, four, five,
Catch a mouse alive!
Six, seven, eight, nine, ten,
Set it free again!

## What the Little Boy Said

One,
Two,
Three.
Come with me!

Four,
Five,
Six.
Look, new chicks!

Seven,
Eight,
Nine.
I wish that they were mine...

Ten,
Ten,
Ten.
They belong to Mother Hen!

## Counting by Twos

Two, four, six, eight,
Counting by twos
Is really great!

Five, ten, fifteen, twenty,
Counting by fives
Will give you plenty!

Twenty, thirty, forty, fifty,
Counting by tens
Is super-nifty!

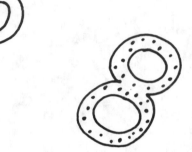

### A Dozen

Twelve things make a dozen.
(I learned that from my cousin!)

A dozen cookies,
A dozen eggs.

Together, two bugs have
At least a dozen legs!

# How Many Legs?

A starfish has five legs,
A spider has eight.

I have only two legs,
(That's why I'm always late.)

A cow has four legs,
A pig and a horse.

Dogs have four legs,
So do cats, of course!

Flies have six legs,
And so do tiny ants.

Centipedes have so many legs,
They'll never learn to dance!

A snail has just one leg,
But always makes do.

A snake has none at all—
Guess I'm lucky to have two!

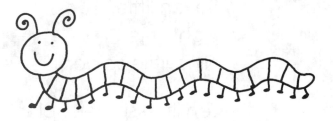

## Person Parts

A person has:
Two eyes,
Two ears,
One mouth,
One nose,
Two hands,
Two feet,
Ten fingers,
Ten toes!

## Little Spiders

One little,
Two little,
Three little spiders,

Four little,
Five little,
Six little spiders,

Seven little,
Eight little,
Nine little spiders,

Ten little spiders spinning webs!

# Giant Dinos

One giant,
Two giant,
Three giant dinos,

Four giant,
Five giant,
Six giant dinos,

Seven giant,
Eight giant,
Nine giant dinos,

Ten giant dinos dining out!

# Mighty Readers

One mighty,
Two mighty,
Three mighty readers!

Four mighty,
Five mighty,
Six mighty readers!

Seven mighty,
Eight mighty,
Nine mighty readers,

Ten mighty readers reading books!

## There Are Two Wheels on a Bike

There are two wheels on a bike,
And three on a trike.
Cars and vans, they each have four.
And trucks, sometimes, have even more!

## One Hundred Days

When I've been in school
One hundred days,

I'll know how to think
One hundred ways.

I will have learned
One hundred facts,

And I'll have eaten
One hundred snacks!

# You Can't Count Every Ladybug

You can't count all the grains of sand
In the oceans and the seas.
You can't count every cat and dog
Or all the forests' trees.

You can't count all the rocks and shells
Or the stars that light the sky.
You can't count every ladybug—
So don't you even try!

## Lots and Lots of People

Lots of folks live in a town,
More than I can count!
But over in the city—
There's ten times that amount!

# When I Was a Baby

When I was a baby
I was toothless and bald.
At first I just lay there,
But later on I crawled.

I finally stood up
And I started to walk.
My goos and gurgles
Soon turned into talk.

I was clever and cute,
So I've been told,
With my rosy cheeks
And bright curls of gold.

Now I am tall,
Good-looking, and smart
I have more teeth
And my hair has a part.

I can even ride a bike
And do all kinds of tricks—
Don't forget to take a picture
Now that I am six!

## Growing

I get taller every day
Although I hardly know it.
But people say, "My, how you've grown!"
So somehow I must show it.

## Look What I Drew!

That crayon person's me.
That other one is you.
I put them side by side,
I pasted them with glue.

I drew me with a happy face,
A grin from ear to ear.
'Cause that is how I always feel
When you, my friend, are near!

## Haircut

It's fun to get a haircut
And sit in the barber chair.
It makes me feel important
To sit so tall up there.

I think it sort of tickles
When they cut and comb my hair
And I look so spiffy special
When I get down from that chair!

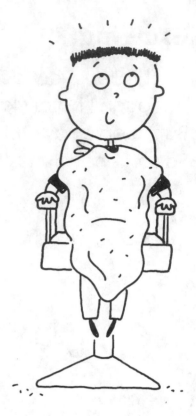

## One or Two

I like myself.
I like me fine.
I play alone
A lot of the time.

I like you, too.
I like you fine.
We play together
A lot of the time.

I play alone.
I play with you.
Fun can be had
By one or two!

## Pocket Treasure

A tiny bit of eggshell
From an empty robin's nest.

It's like a piece of summer sky,
The blue that I like best.

Four fine rocks, one perfect shell,
A rusty little locket—

Those are just a few of the things
In my blue-jeans pocket!

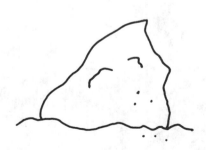

## To Be Six

I can say the alphabet
Right through from A to Z.

And print my name, so nice and neat—
Do you want to see?

I can count
By ones and twos,

Ride a bike
And tie my shoes.

It's super duper
To be six—

So tall and smart
And full of tricks!

## Smiles Go 'Round

I like to smile.
I like to grin.
I like to be happy-hearted.
'Cause smiles and grins and happiness
Seem to come back to where they started!

## The Race

I like to run,
I like to race.
Today I did my best.
And I was so much faster
Than I ever would've guessed.

When they said "START"
I moved so fast
I thought that I might burst.
But I huffed and puffed and tried so hard—
I crossed the finish FIRST!

## Eyes to See

What luck that we have eyes to see:
The morning light,
The stars at night,
The blueness of the sea.

What luck that we have eyes to see:
The gentle deer,
Her fawn so near,
All creatures wild and free.

What luck that we have eyes to see:
The sun above,
The ones we love,
How lucky can we be!

## Finger Wise

My fingers tell me oh-so much
Through my amazing sense of touch.

I know what's lumpy,
Smooth, or bumpy—
What is cold or hot.
I know when something's prickly.
I know when something's not.

Fuzzy, furry, shiny, grainy,
Warm and cuddly, icy, rainy.

All this I sense without my eyes
Because my fingers are so wise!

## The Nose Knows

We think that we TASTE flavors
But it simply isn't so.
Chocolate or vanilla—
The tongue just doesn't know.

We tell flavors 'cause we SMELL them!
So, close your eyes
And plug your nose. . .
And you will see that this is so!

## I Spy

I spy with my little eye
Something that is red.
It has a stem and thorns and leaves.
It has a velvet head.

It's soft to touch
And sweet to smell.
So. . .now what is it?
Can you tell?

Answer: a rose

## Sounds All Around

Chicks on the farm go, "PEEP, PEEP, PEEP!"
Horns in the city scream, "BEEP, BEEP, BEEP!"

A leaky faucet says, "PLINK, PLINK, PLINK!"
Coins in my pocket chant, "CLINK, CLINK, CLINK!"

The wind in the field whispers, "SWISH, SWISH, SWISH!"
Soaking wet sneakers squeak, "SQUISH, SQUISH, SQUISH!"

So many sounds: PLINK, SQUISH, ROAR!
So many sounds, can you think of more?

# Home Sweet Home

People live in houses
In many lands and places,
As different from each other
As their many names and faces.

There are houses made of mud and grass,
Of bricks, of snow, of stones.
There are houses round and houses square
And houses shaped like cones.

Some people live in motor homes,
They wander and they roam.
And whatever place they choose to park—
They call it home sweet home!

## A Trip to the Zoo

The zoo is an amazing place—
Where tigers yawn and lions pace.

Where monkeys swing and pandas climb,
Where peacocks strut and snakes unwind.

Where sleepy elephants chomp on hay.
Where seals and otters play and play.

So many animals BIG and small—
I love to watch them one and all!

# I'd Like to Have a Treehouse

I'd like to have a treehouse,
High so high.
I could be a king there,
Eating a cherry pie!

I'd like to have a treehouse,
High so high.
I could visit birds there,
Look them in the eye!

I'd like to have a treehouse,
High so high.
I could be a dreamer,
And watch the clouds sail by!

I'd like to have a treehouse,
High so high,
We could drink our tea there—
Only you and I!

## Paul and Pete and Patty, Too

Paul and Pete and Patty, too.
We have so many things to do!
We go to the store.
We go to the zoo,
Paul and Pete and Patty, too!

We like to paint.
We like to bake.
We eat a pizza pie we make.
We decorate a birthday cake.
We ride our bikes out to the lake.

We're never short of things to do,
Paul and Pete and Patty, too!

## Sandbox

I like to play in the sandbox
With a little truck and a car.
I build hills and towns and sandy streets,
Then pretend I'm driving far!

## At the Pool

The swimming pool is packed today.
The kids all splish and splash and play.

They swim underwater!
They jump from the side!
They dive off the board!
They zip down the slide!

There are flippers and goggles
And snorkels and floats!
There are tubes and rings
And beachballs and boats!

A splishy splashy day in the pool
Is the greatest way of keeping cool!

## Bikes and Trikes

There are
Bikes
And trikes
And scooters.
There are
Roller-skates
And wagons.
All are great for children,
But not so good for dragons!

## Did You See the Jet Plane?

Did you see the jet plane's,
Trail across the sky?

Did you see the freight train,
As it clattered by?

Did you see the motorboat,
Puttering about?

Did you see the firetruck,
And hear its siren shout?

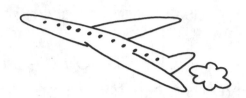

## So Big, So Small

When you climb aboard a jumbo jet
It seems so huge inside.
It's a long way to the bathroom
And it's more than ten seats wide!

But when you lie in a meadow
And a jumbo jet goes by,
It looks just like a tiny bird
Humming through the sky!

## Wheels on a Train

A train has wheels of steel
That are very, very strong.
And it can have a hundred wheels
If it's very, very long!

## Breakfast on the Farm

Jersey cow, if you please,
Give us cream to make some cheese,
Jersey cow, don't moo and mutter,
Give us cream to make some butter!

Little chicken, if you please,
Give us eggs for an omelet (cheese!).
Little chicken, if you are able,
Give us eggs for the morning table!

## At the Grocery Store

You'll see apples
And corn and lemon pie,
Pickles and peaches,
My oh my!
Peanut butter, jam,
All kinds of meats—
And don't forget
The ice-cream treats!

# A Trip to the Fruit Stand

Apples, grapefruit, berries blue.
Oranges, lemons, peaches, too.

Bananas, cherries, the fruit stand sells,
Coconuts in hard brown shells.

Limes and grapes and melons round
Ripe purple plums sold by the pound!

# Fruit Riddle

What's round and shiny, red or green,
The perfect snack for king and queen?

What grows on trees, is sweet or tart,
And holds its seeds inside its heart?

Answer: an apple

## Silly Sandwich

I emptied the fridge,
Left the cupboard bare—
'Cause I built the best sandwich
Seen anywhere!

Salami and pickles,
Lasagna and cheese,
Potato chips and lettuce leaves,
Jelly, cupcakes, ice cream, too—

That silly sandwich grew
And GREW!

It was a feat
For goodness sake!
But now. . .
I have a tummy ache!

## I Really Love My Veggies

I really love my veggies.
I seldom make a fuss.
I only ever draw the line
At cooked asparagus!

## What the Popcorn Said

"POP!"
Said the kernel.
Did you hear it shout?
(It's good we kept the lid on
Or it would've jumped right out!)

Suddenly they all started jumping
What a HOPPING-POPPING RACKET!

As every little kernel
Burst its tiny jacket!

## Pizza Time

My favorite food is pizza.
I could eat it every day.
When someone says, "It's pizza time,"
Don't get in my way!

I love the sauce so spicy.
I love the gooey cheese.
And I can have ten slices
As long as I say, "Please!"

## At the Ice-Cream Shop

Chocolate,
Mango,
Lemon lime,
Mint chip
And cherry,
All look divine!

Flavors and colors
So tempting and yummy.
Now, tell me which one should go
Inside my tummy?

## Ice-Cream Dream

I'd know for sure I was asleep
And in a happy dream
If I asked, "What's for dinner?"
And then Mom said, "Ice cream!"

# Let Me Dream of Peanut Butter

In my bed, I'm known to mutter,
"Let me dream of peanut butter."

Peanut butter with gobs of jelly.
Peanut butter inside my belly.

Peanut butter on toast with jam
Peanut butter with pickles and ham.

Wait a minute—That's not right. . .
Wake me up before I bite!

## Do You Have a Pet?

Do you have a bird
That sits upon your head?
Do you have a cat
That crawls into your bed?

Do you have a gerbil
That runs around a wheel?
Do you have a dog
That you've taught how to heel?

Do you have a bunny
That lives inside a hutch?
Do you have a turtle
That doesn't move too much?

Do you have a fish
That gets fed by your mother?
Do you have a snake
That scares your little brother?

## My Cousin Has White Mice

My cousin has white mice
With little pink eyes.
My friend has a lizard
That eats only flies.

Every kid I know
Wants some kind of pet.
If there are some who don't. . .
I haven't met them yet!

## Bear-ly Awake

If you were really sleepy,
Do you think you'd choose
To snore and snore the weeks away
In a long, long winter snooze?

Bears do snuggle in cozy dens
And sleep the winter away.
Then little cubs, a few weeks old,
Come out in spring to play!

## Summer Bunny, Winter Bunny

A summer bunny's brown
Except for his nose,
But a winter bunny's white
If he lives where it snows.
(And his coat hides him well
Wherever he goes!)

## Dog, Bird, Turtle, Bat

I love to look at animals
In books and on TV.

In fact, there's not one animal
That doesn't interest me:

Dog, bird, turtle, bat,
Mouse, mole, fish, cat,

Panda, horse, peacock so fine,
Penguin, parrot, porcupine,

Tiger, goat, giraffe so tall,
Flea and fly and beetle small,

Lizard, blue jay, lion, fox,
Plus everything else that flies or walks!

# Farm Families

A mother sheep is called an ewe
The father is a ram.
The little newborn baby
Is what we call a lamb.

A mother pig is called a sow,
The father is a boar.
A litter of new piglets
Can number ten or more.

A mother cow is called just that,
The father is a bull.
The baby calf is hungry
And drinks 'til it is full.

A mother horse is called a mare,
The father is the sire.
The little colt on racing legs
Just never seems to tire.

A mother goat is called a nanny,
The father is a billy.
The little goat is called a kid.
Now, doesn't that seem silly!

## Farm Riddles

"Peep, peep, peep!"
It's morning on the farm.
Who's that waking up
Inside the big, red barn?

Answer: a chick

"Oink, oink, oink!"
It's morning on the farm.
Who's that waking up
Inside the big, red barn?

Answer: a pig

"Baa, baa, baa!"
It's morning on the farm.
Who's that waking up
Inside the big, red barn?

Answer: a lamb

# More Farm Riddles

"Neigh, neigh, neigh!"
It's morning on the farm.
Who's that waking up
Inside the big, red barn?

Answer: a horse

"Moo, moo, moo!"
It's morning on the farm.
Who's that waking up
Inside the big, red barn?

Answer: a cow

"Cock-a-doodle-do!"
It's morning on the farm.
Who's that waking up
Inside the big, red barn?

Answer: a rooster

## Five Little Ducklings

Five little ducklings
Floating in a line,
Stick close to mother
Almost all the time.

Five silver minnows
Flashing to and fro,
Playing tag beneath them
Where the green reeds grow.

## Green, Green Frog

Green green frog
On a brown brown log.

You wait for a fly
To come buzz buzz by.

Your tongue's so quick
When you give it a flick—

It's bye-bye Mr. Fly!

# I Spy

I spy with my little eye
Something that can scurry.
Something grey, something brown,
Something super furry.
Something timid, something meek.
Something that makes folks say, "Eeeeeeeeeek!"

This something's favorite food is cheese . . .
So tell me now the answer, please!

Answer: a mouse

## Little Mouse, Little Mouse

Little mouse,
Little mouse,
Your watchful eyes are shiny.

Little mouse,
If you have a house
It must be very tiny!

## The Robin's Secret

Outside my window
In the backyard trees,

A robin's tune drifts
On the morning breeze.

But hard as I try
I just can't see

Where she is hiding
In that thick maple tree!

## Pelican Pouch

The pelican has a bill
That's built to carry fish
So she never has to bother with
A pocket, purse, or dish.

## The Peacock's Tail

The peacock's tail is a beautiful fan
All shades of blue and green.

A grand surprise
With spots like eyes
And gold threads in between.

With his tail spread out
He struts about
As if before the queen!

## Tadpoles

Tadpoles start as
Clusters of eggs. . .

Then heads and tails
And pretty soon legs.

Next thing you know
They all are on logs. . .

And croaking away
As full-grown frogs!

# Mom's Allergic

I'm not allowed to keep the snake
'Cause Mom's allergic for goodness sake!

It comes to me as some surprise
That snakes cause sneezing
And watery eyes.

I've told her this snake
Is perfectly harmless.
It's clawless, it's toothless,
It's stingless, it's armless!

And to help make my point
This snake is not charmless:
It's quiet, it's pretty,
It's dry to the touch.
It's gentle, it's friendly,
It doesn't eat much.

Aw, what the heck,
I know it's no use.
(This allergy thing
Is some fancy excuse!)

## Animal Homes

A hive is home
To the fuzzy bumblebee.

A bird has a nest
In the branches of a tree.

An ant lives in soil
That is shaped into a mound.

A beaver builds a lodge
To keep babies safe and sound.

A mouse lives in a granary,
A barn, or a shack.

And a snail carts his home
Right upon his back!

# A Dinosaur Was at My Door

A dinosaur was at my door.
He said he'd come for lunch.

And so I said, "Do come right in—
I've some veggies you can munch!"

He ate cabbage and corn
And tomatoes and beans.

And spinach and lettuce
And lots of fresh greens.

He had broccoli, beet tops,
Zucchini, and such.

He ate turnips and parsnips
And squash (not too much!).

He ate onions, cucumber,
Kale, and tomatoes.

Celery, carrots,
Mushrooms, potatoes. . .

"Are you almost full?"
I asked him politely.

"I've saved room for dessert,"
He answered me brightly!

# Beetle Has His Beetle Ways

Beetle has his beetle ways,
Beetle friends, beetle days.

Beetle climbs up
Plants and rocks,
Never wearing shoes and socks!

Beetle loves exploring things,
(He sometimes spread his beetle wings.)

You can watch him,
All you like—
Busy little beetle tyke!

But please don't take a beetle home,
'Cause beetles do so like to roam!

# Butterfly, Flutter By

Butterfly, flutter by,
On little painted wings!
Butterfly, flutter by,
One of my favorite things!
Butterfly, flutter by,
On your lovely painted wings.

## Caterpillar Small

Green and yellow,
Green and yellow,
Caterpillar small.

In my hand you curl up
In a fuzzy, furry ball.

Green and yellow,
Green and yellow,
Caterpillar small.

I'll put you back in the tall, tall grass
And not hurt you at all!

# Summer Surprise

Winking, blinking
Teeny-tiny lights—
Fireflies speaking
On hot summer nights!

# Mr. Bumblebee

Black and yellow
Fuzzy fellow,
Mr. Bumblebee.

Black and yellow
Busy fellow,
Honey, you're for me!

## I Spy

I spy with my little eye
Something in the grass.

It jumps and hops and chews up crops,
You hear it as you pass.

It plays a tune
On its legs like a fiddle
Can you tell me now
the answer to my riddle?

Answer: a cricket

## I Spy

I spy with my little eye
Something black and yellow.

He visits flowers in the yard—
This fuzzy, wuzzy fellow!

He buzzes, stings, has tiny wings,
Makes something for our table.

If you can't guess the answer now,
You never will be able!

Answer: a bee

## The Tiny World

Tiny beetle, busy and black!
Spider creeping across a crack!
Ladybug dressed in a spotted shell!
Grasshopper green, you hide so well!
Wiggly worm in a robin's beak!
Dragonfly buzzing over the creek!
All so tiny, all so small—
To you, I must seem VERY tall!

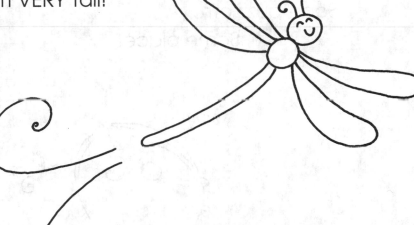

## The Ladybug's Coat

The ladybug's coat
Has spots of black—
What fine polka-dots
She wears on her back!

I've a little red coat
Almost like that—
But it's missing those pretty
Spots of black!

## Mosquito

Mosquito whining by my ear,
I can't sleep when you are near!

You buzz and hover by my head,
You circle 'round and 'round my bed!

I pull the covers over my face
And hope you'll
           Soon buzz off
                    Some place!

## Spider Friends

Spiders, spiders,
On silky threads—
You decorate drab corners
With lovely, lacy webs!

## Webs in the Grass

When spider webs are hung with dew
They magically come into view.

Like pixie tents in morning grass,
Like shining nets of silver glass.

But when the sun is hot and bright,
Those webs are hidden from our sight

Like stars that seem to fade away—
Invisible in the light of day!

## Wiggly Worm

Wiggly Worm
Oh, how you squirm
When I see you in the garden!

Wiggly Worm
If I laugh as you squirm
I do so beg your pardon!